Spotter's Guide to

HORSES & PONIES

Joanna Spector

Illustrated by David Wright,
Elaine Keenan & Malcolm McGregor

with additional illustrations by
Ed Roberts and Andy Martin

Puffin Books

Contents

Edited by Tim Dowley and Felicity Mansfield

First published in 1979 by
Usborne Publishing Limited,
20 Garrick Street, London WC2
Published in Puffin Books 1980

Printed and Bound in Great Britain by
Hazell Watson & Viney Ltd, Aylesbury, Bucks

How to use this book

This book is an identification guide to breeds of horses and ponies from all over the world. Take it with you when you go to shows, riding stables, racecourses or any place that you might see horses.

The breeds are arranged with ponies first, followed by riding horses, harness horses and draught horses.

Next to each picture is a short description of the breed, telling you where the breed comes from, what kind of work it does, the colours it can be, and its height. It also points out any special details about the breed.

Some of the colours have unusual names. You can look them up on page 7. If there are any other words you don't understand, look them up in the glossary on page 58, or find them on the diagram showing the parts of a horse on page 49.

Scorecard

There is a small blank circle next to each description. When you see a breed, make a tick in the circle. You will be able to find many of the breeds in this book all over Britain. Others live either in particular areas of the country, or in other countries, so they will be harder to find. Others are very rare indeed; you will probably see them only in zoos. The scorecard at the end of the book gives a score for each breed you see. A common breed scores 5 points, and a very rare one 25 points. You can tick off very rare breeds if you see them in a film or on television.

Height

The height of horses and ponies is measured in hands, from the ground to the top of the withers. One hand equals 4 inches (10 centimetres). If the description says that a horse is 15.2 hh, for example, it means that the horse is 15 hands and 2 inches high (hh means "hands high"). Ponies are usually less than 14.2 hh.

Withers

Height is measured in hands

Tick off each horse or pony when you have seen it

3

How horses began

Arab horse

Exmoor pony

The first horse looked rather like a deer. It lived in forests and woodlands, 50 million years ago. Gradually, different types of horses began to appear. They all became fast and sure footed, because they had to be able to run away from their enemies.

All the breeds we know today are descended from two ancient types of horses – the southern type, from the hot deserts of North Africa and southern Asia, and the northern type, from cold, hilly or mountainous parts of Europe and Asia.

The southern type had a fine, silky coat and light bones. It could run fast and survive on small amounts of food. It was similar to the Arab horse of today. The northern type had a thick, rough coat and sturdy legs. It lived off poor, scrubby grass and bushes. This type was similar to breeds like the Przewalski and Exmoor of today. Several thousand years ago, in Europe, man began to control the development of horses like these. There are now about 200 different breeds of horses and ponies.

Wild Horses

The only truly wild breed left in the world is the Przewalski, from the Gobi Desert in Mongolia, where some still live in wild herds.

The Przewalski

How horses are used

To begin with, horses were hunted for food. Later on they were bred to do all sorts of work. Harness horses, for example, pull light carts and carriages, while draught horses are used for ploughing and haulage (pulling heavy carts and wagons). Today, people ride mostly for pleasure or sport, although some horses still work on farms, especially in eastern Europe.

Heavy draught horse pulling a plough

▼ In the 19th century, three Arab stallions were crossed with English hunters to produce the Thoroughbred, the finest riding horse ever bred. It gets its qualities of speed, good looks and endurance from the Arab.

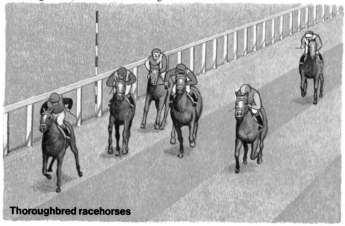

Thoroughbred racehorses

Looking at horses

At first, it is difficult to tell what breed a horse or pony is, but after a while, it becomes easier. Here are some clues to help you:

Welsh pony

If the horse carries its tail high and has a dished profile (a face that curves in), it probably has some Arab blood. It may be an Anglo-Arab, or even a Welsh pony.

Highland pony

If it is small and sturdy, with a long, rough coat, it is probably a mountain or moorland pony – perhaps a Highland or Dartmoor pony.

Thoroughbred

If the horse is tall, with long legs, a fine skin and coat, and a light build, it is probably a Thoroughbred.

Percheron

If it is big, heavy and slow, with feather (long hairs) around its fetlocks, it is probably a draught horse, like a Percheron or a Shire.

Where to look

Many of the horses you see are likely to be cross bred. It can be fun trying to guess which different breeds their ancestors were. Look for pure bred horses and ponies at:

● Horse shows, where there are classes for various breeds.

● Stud farms, where horses are bred. (This is probably the best place to find pure breeds.)

● The breed's natural surroundings. For example, hills and moors in Britain, lowlands in France and Belgium, mountains in Austria.

● Racing stables or racecourses (these are the best places to see Thoroughbreds).

● Riding stables. At the Spanish Riding School in Vienna, for example, you will see only Lipizzaners.

Ask at your nearest riding school if any of their horses or ponies are pure bred.

Colours and markings

Most breeds are the common colours – bay, brown, chestnut and grey. Some are always a particular colour. For example, the Fjord pony is always dun.

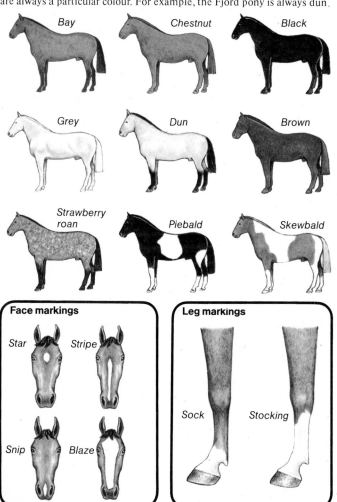

Bay

Chestnut

Black

Grey

Dun

Brown

Strawberry roan

Piebald

Skewbald

Face markings

Star

Stripe

Snip

Blaze

Leg markings

Sock

Stocking

Ponies

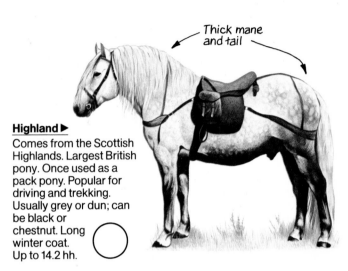

Thick mane and tail

Highland ▶

Comes from the Scottish Highlands. Largest British pony. Once used as a pack pony. Popular for driving and trekking. Usually grey or dun; can be black or chestnut. Long winter coat. Up to 14.2 hh.

Short, strong neck

◀ Shetland

Smallest British pony. Once used to carry peat. Popular as pet for riding and driving. Usually black, brown or chestnut. Can be piebald or skewbald. About 9.2 hh.

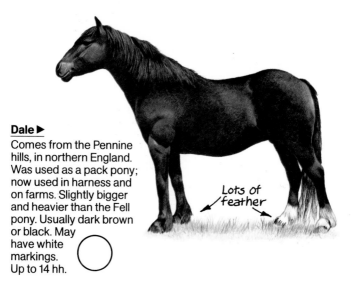

Dale ▶

Comes from the Pennine hills, in northern England. Was used as a pack pony; now used in harness and on farms. Slightly bigger and heavier than the Fell pony. Usually dark brown or black. May have white markings. Up to 14 hh.

Lots of feather

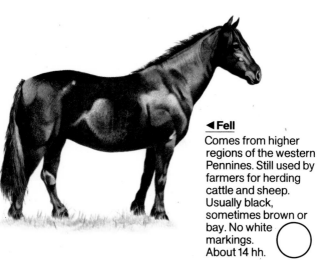

◀ Fell

Comes from higher regions of the western Pennines. Still used by farmers for herding cattle and sheep. Usually black, sometimes brown or bay. No white markings. About 14 hh.

Light-coloured muzzle

Rough, springy coat

Exmoor ▶
Oldest breed in Britain. Several herds still live half wild on Exmoor, in southwest England. Hardy and strong willed. Good riding ponies for children. Bay or brown with light coloured underside. Up to 12.3 hh.

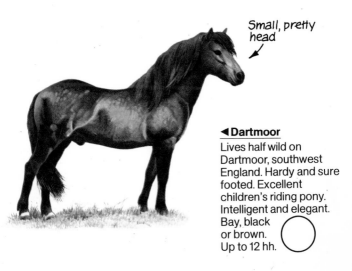

Small, pretty head

◀ Dartmoor
Lives half wild on Dartmoor, southwest England. Hardy and sure footed. Excellent children's riding pony. Intelligent and elegant. Bay, black or brown. Up to 12 hh.

New Forest ▶

Lives in the New Forest, in southern England. Very hardy. Good riding pony. Can be various shapes. Any colour except piebald or skewbald. 12-14 hh.

Long neck

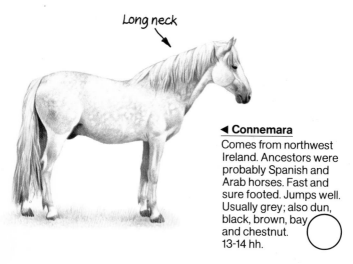

◀ Connemara

Comes from northwest Ireland. Ancestors were probably Spanish and Arab horses. Fast and sure footed. Jumps well. Usually grey; also dun, black, brown, bay and chestnut. 13-14 hh.

11

Arab-type head

Tail carried high

Welsh Mountain ▶
Old breed from Wales with
Arab and Thoroughbred
blood. Popular show pony
for riding and driving. Safe
for children. Usually grey
or chestnut; can be any
colour except
piebald or
skewbald.
Up to 12 hh.

Arched
neck

Feather

◀ Welsh Cob
Cross bred from Welsh
ponies and Andalusian
horses. Strong; a good
trotter. Often driven in
harness. Most colours
except piebald
or skewbald.
14-15 hh.

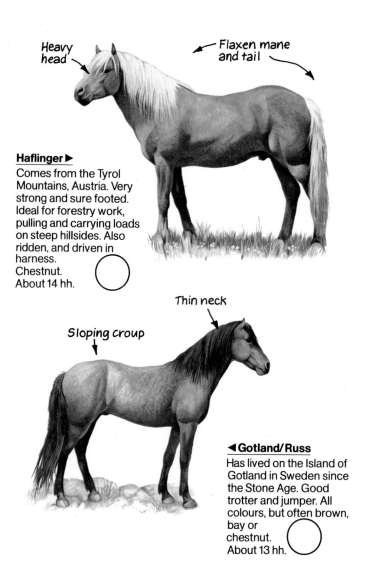

Heavy head

Flaxen mane and tail

Haflinger ▶

Comes from the Tyrol Mountains, Austria. Very strong and sure footed. Ideal for forestry work, pulling and carrying loads on steep hillsides. Also ridden, and driven in harness.
Chestnut.
About 14 hh.

Thin neck

Sloping croup

◀ Gotland/Russ

Has lived on the Island of Gotland in Sweden since the Stone Age. Good trotter and jumper. All colours, but often brown, bay or chestnut.
About 13 hh.

Icelandic ▶

Bred from various northern
European ponies. Used as
riding or pack pony.
Some are bred to eat.
Quiet and friendly. Any
colour; often grey, dun,
brown, black or
chestnut.
12-13 hh.

High
knee
action ←

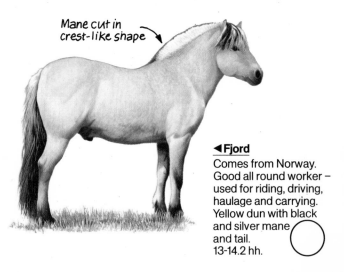

Mane cut in
crest-like shape ↘

◀ Fjord

Comes from Norway.
Good all round worker –
used for riding, driving,
haulage and carrying.
Yellow dun with black
and silver mane
and tail.
13-14.2 hh.

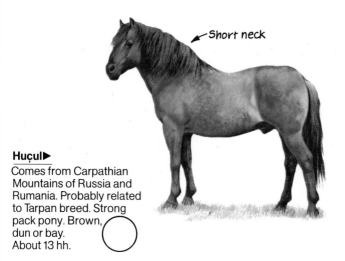

←Short neck

Huçul▶
Comes from Carpathian Mountains of Russia and Rumania. Probably related to Tarpan breed. Strong pack pony. Brown, dun or bay.
About 13 hh.

◀Kazakh
Comes from Russia. Good long distance racing pony. Mares' milk used to make a fermented drink called "kumis". Any colour; often bay, brown or chestnut.
About 13 hh.

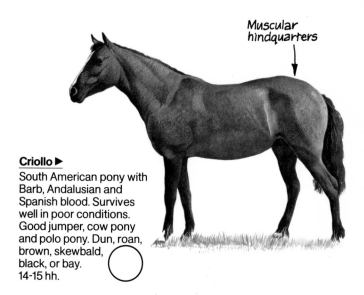

Muscular
hindquarters

Criollo ▶

South American pony with
Barb, Andalusian and
Spanish blood. Survives
well in poor conditions.
Good jumper, cow pony
and polo pony. Dun, roan,
brown, skewbald,
black, or bay.
14-15 hh.

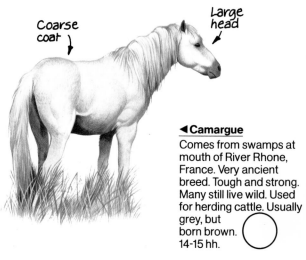

Coarse
coat

Large
head

◀ Camargue

Comes from swamps at
mouth of River Rhone,
France. Very ancient
breed. Tough and strong.
Many still live wild. Used
for herding cattle. Usually
grey, but
born brown.
14-15 hh.

Long, silky coat

Falabella ▶
Comes from Argentina.
A miniature horse;
not very strong. Good
natured; popular
children's pet and
driving pony.
Any colour.
Less than 7 hh.

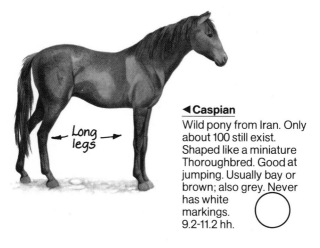

Long legs

◀ Caspian
Wild pony from Iran. Only
about 100 still exist.
Shaped like a miniature
Thoroughbred. Good at
jumping. Usually bay or
brown; also grey. Never
has white
markings.
9.2-11.2 hh.

17

Coarse mane and coat

Tarpan ▶
Oldest breed in Europe
and northern Asia. Was
once hunted for food. Two
wild herds live in forests in
Poland. Very hardy.
Usually light brown with
black ears, mane,
tail, and legs.
About 13 hh.

Upright mane

Large head

Thin
tail

◀ Przewalski
Also called Asiatic or
Mongolian Wild Horse.
Unchanged since the Ice
Age. Only about 300 exist,
some in zoos, others in
herds in Gobi Desert,
Mongolia. Bay or
dun colour.
12-14 hh.

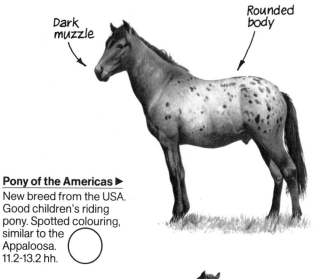

Dark
muzzle

Rounded
body

Pony of the Americas ▶
New breed from the USA.
Good children's riding
pony. Spotted colouring,
similar to the
Appaloosa.
11.2-13.2 hh.

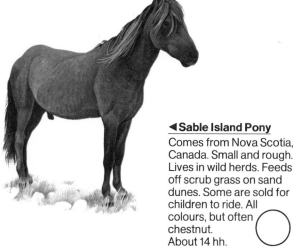

◀ Sable Island Pony
Comes from Nova Scotia,
Canada. Small and rough.
Lives in wild herds. Feeds
off scrub grass on sand
dunes. Some are sold for
children to ride. All
colours, but often
chestnut.
About 14 hh.

19

Riding Horses

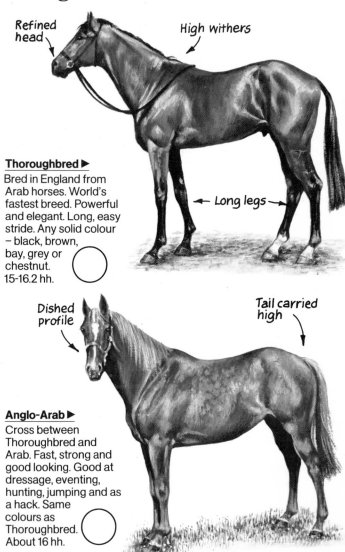

Refined head

High withers

Thoroughbred ▶
Bred in England from Arab horses. World's fastest breed. Powerful and elegant. Long, easy stride. Any solid colour – black, brown, bay, grey or chestnut. 15-16.2 hh.

Long legs

Dished profile

Tail carried high

Anglo-Arab ▶
Cross between Thoroughbred and Arab. Fast, strong and good looking. Good at dressage, eventing, hunting, jumping and as a hack. Same colours as Thoroughbred. About 16 hh.

High tail

American Saddlebred ▶

Once used by families in southern states of the USA as a riding and harness horse. Has three to five ambling gaits (paces). Smooth, effortless ride. Bay, brown, or chestnut. 15-15.3 hh.

High knee action

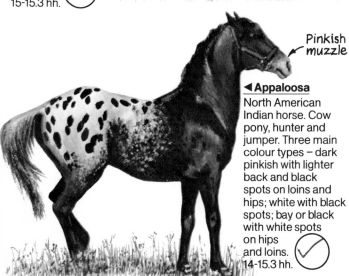

Pinkish muzzle

◀ Appaloosa

North American Indian horse. Cow pony, hunter and jumper. Three main colour types – dark pinkish with lighter back and black spots on loins and hips; white with black spots; bay or black with white spots on hips and loins. 14-15.3 hh.

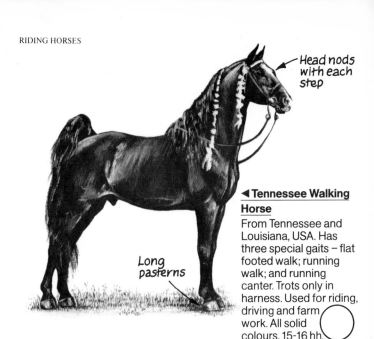

Head nods
with each
step

Long
pasterns

◄ Tennessee Walking Horse

From Tennessee and Louisiana, USA. Has three special gaits – flat footed walk; running walk; and running canter. Trots only in harness. Used for riding, driving and farm work. All solid colours. 15-16 hh.

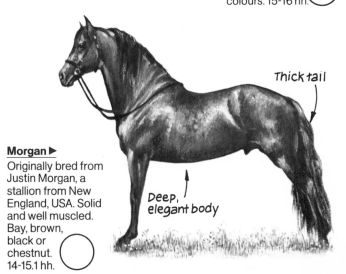

Thick tail

Deep,
elegant body

Morgan ►

Originally bred from Justin Morgan, a stallion from New England, USA. Solid and well muscled. Bay, brown, black or chestnut. 14-15.1 hh.

Powerful hindquarters

Quarter Horse ▶
Comes from the
USA. Named after
quarter mile races.
Used on ranches as
a cow pony and at
rodeos. Quick and
intelligent.
Any colour.
15-16 hh.

Short neck

Sloping croup

◀ Paso Fino
American breed
descended from
horses of Spanish
explorers. Has five
extra gaits. Doesn't
trot. Some do
special, slow "paso
fino" gait.
Any colour.
13-15.2 hh.

23

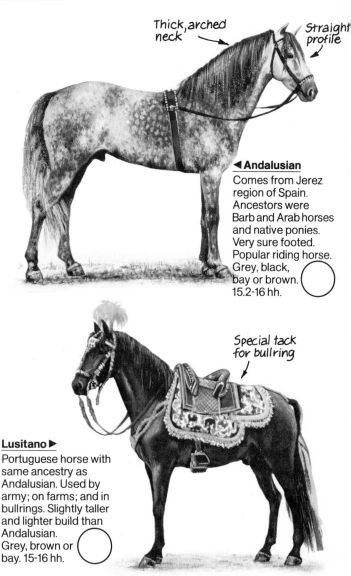

Thick, arched neck

Straight profile

◄ Andalusian
Comes from Jerez region of Spain. Ancestors were Barb and Arab horses and native ponies. Very sure footed. Popular riding horse. Grey, black, bay or brown. 15.2-16 hh.

Special tack for bullring

Lusitano ►
Portuguese horse with same ancestry as Andalusian. Used by army; on farms; and in bullrings. Slightly taller and lighter build than Andalusian. Grey, brown or bay. 15-16 hh.

24

Small, fine head with dished profile

Tail carried high

Shagya Arab ▶
A type of Arab from
eastern Europe. Can
live on little or poor
food. Tireless.
Popular as a cavalry
horse in World War
One. Usually
grey.
14-15 hh.

Longish back

Large eyes

◀ Polish Arab
Another type of Arab.
Bred in Poland since
1500. Used as a
racehorse. Very tough
and strong. Many
exported to England
and the USA. Can be
bay, grey or
chestnut.
14.2-15.1 hh.

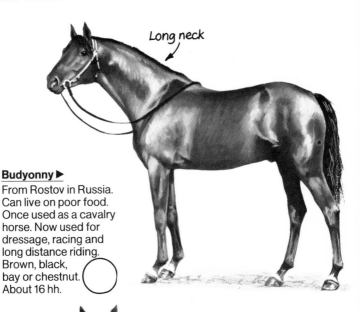

Long neck

Budyonny ▶
From Rostov in Russia.
Can live on poor food.
Once used as a cavalry
horse. Now used for
dressage, racing and
long distance riding.
Brown, black,
bay or chestnut.
About 16 hh.

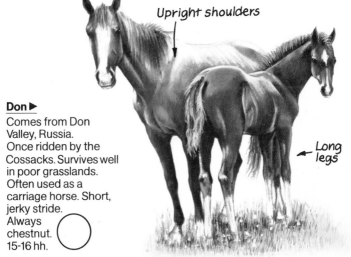

Upright shoulders

Long legs

Don ▶
Comes from Don
Valley, Russia.
Once ridden by the
Cossacks. Survives well
in poor grasslands.
Often used as a
carriage horse. Short,
jerky stride.
Always
chestnut.
15-16 hh.

High, narrow body

Fine coat
with metallic
sheen

Akhal-Teke ▶
Ancient breed from
Turkoman Steppes,
Russia. Used for
jumping, racing,
dressage and long
distance riding. Can
stand great heat or
cold. Golden
chestnut, bay, black
or grey.
About
15.1 hh.

Fine, thin
tail

◀ Karabair
Comes from the
mountains of central
Asia. Can work in dry,
hot weather. Fast and
good natured.
Grey, bay
or chestnut.
14.2-15.2 hh.

27

Often has
white face
markings

◄ Palomino

Popular in USA.
Descended from
Arab horses.
Classed either as a
breed or a colour.
Most are bred for
shows. Some jump
and hunt. Any shade
of chestnut, with
white mane
and tail.
14-16 hh.

overo
marking type

Pinto ►

Bred in USA. Used for
riding and herding. Two
marking types: overo—
white areas begin on
underside and extend
upwards in an irregular
pattern; tobiano—white
starts on back and
spreads downwards
usually in a regular
pattern.
Various
heights.

28

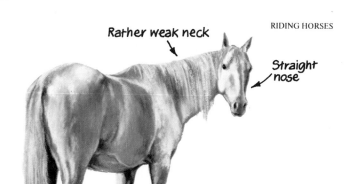

Rather weak neck

Straight nose

◀ Turkoman
Comes from
Turkoman Steppes,
in northern Iran.
Strong and tireless.
Good riding horse.
Usually grey or bay;
but also dun
or chestnut.
14.3-15.2 hh.

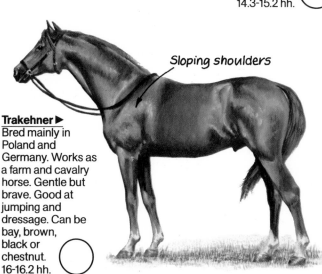

Sloping shoulders

Trakehner ▶
Bred mainly in
Poland and
Germany. Works as
a farm and cavalry
horse. Gentle but
brave. Good at
jumping and
dressage. Can be
bay, brown,
black or
chestnut.
16-16.2 hh.

Ram-shaped head

Anglo Norman ▶

Cross bred in England from big war horses brought over by William the Conqueror. Brave and strong. Good riding and jumping horse. Often chestnut. 15.2-16.3 hh.

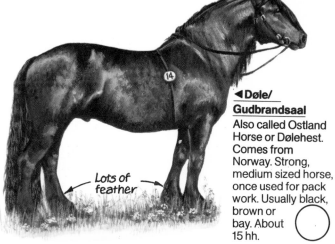

Lots of feather

◀ Døle/ Gudbrandsaal

Also called Ostland Horse or Dølehest. Comes from Norway. Strong, medium sized horse, once used for pack work. Usually black, brown or bay. About 15 hh.

Strong
hindquarters

Heavy
shoulders

◄ Hanoverian
German breed
descended from
war horses ridden in
Middle Ages. Strong.
Good show jumper.
Any solid colour;
often bay
or brown.
16-17 hh.

Holstein ►
Bred in marshes of
River Elbe, West
Germany. Big and
strong. Good
carriage horse and
show jumper.
Usually brown,
bay or
black.
16-16.2 hh.

Knabstrup ▶

Danish breed descended from a spotted Spanish mare. Popular as a circus horse. Fast and hardy. Always spotted. Usually white with black spots. About 15 hh.

Short, arched neck

Lipizzaner ▶

Austria's famous breed, used by the Spanish Riding School in Vienna. Bred from Andalusian horses. Excellent dressage horse; also good in harness. Born brown or black, changes to grey. Pure white in old age. 14.3-16 hh.

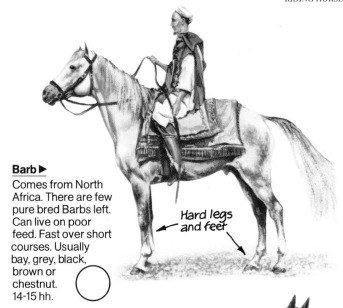

Barb ▶

Comes from North
Africa. There are few
pure bred Barbs left.
Can live on poor
feed. Fast over short
courses. Usually
bay, grey, black,
brown or
chestnut.
14-15 hh.

Hard legs
and feet

Narrow
hindquarters

High withers

◀ Waler

First bred in New
South Wales,
Australia. Former
cavalry horse, now
herds cattle on
ranches. Also used
at rodeos, for show
jumping and general
riding. Any
solid colour.
15-16 hh.

33

Harness Horses

◄ Standardbred
Famous trotting
horse from the USA.
It had to reach a
standard speed to
become registered,
hence the name.
Races in carts called
sulkies. Any solid
colour; usually bay,
black, or
brown.
15-16 hh.

Long back

Orlov Trotter ►
Comes from Russia,
and named after
Count Orlov. Strong
and quite heavy;
once used by
cavalry. Fairly high
knee action. Often
grey, also
black or bay.
15.2-17 hh.

Some
feather

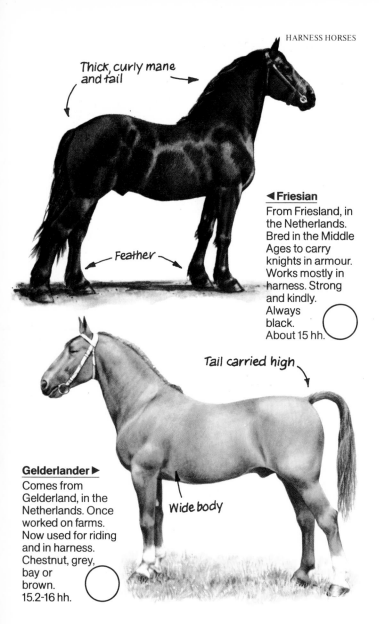

Thick, curly mane and tail →

Feather →

◄ Friesian
From Friesland, in the Netherlands. Bred in the Middle Ages to carry knights in armour. Works mostly in harness. Strong and kindly. Always black. About 15 hh.

Tail carried high ↘

Gelderlander ►
Comes from Gelderland, in the Netherlands. Once worked on farms. Now used for riding and in harness. Chestnut, grey, bay or brown. 15.2-16 hh.

Wide body

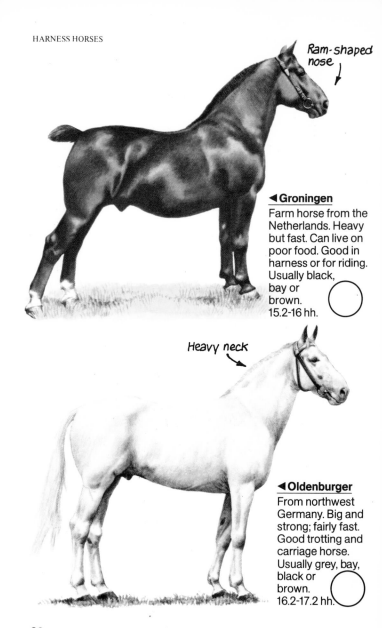

Ram-shaped nose

Heavy neck

◀ **Groningen**

Farm horse from the Netherlands. Heavy but fast. Can live on poor food. Good in harness or for riding. Usually black, bay or brown. 15.2-16 hh.

◀ **Oldenburger**

From northwest Germany. Big and strong; fairly fast. Good trotting and carriage horse. Usually grey, bay, black or brown. 16.2-17.2 hh.

Sloping shoulders

Cleveland Bay ▶
Comes from
Yorkshire, England.
Sure footed, but not
very fast. Used for
carriage work. Good
jumper. Always bay,
without
white
markings.
15-16.2 hh.

High tail   Long back

◀ Hackney
English high stepping
trotter, famous for its
exaggerated but
graceful action. Used
in light carriages,
for showing.
Bay, black
or brown.
14.3-15.3 hh.

Basic type

Kustanair ▶
From Kazakhstan, in
Russia. Good all
rounder. Three sorts:
Steppe – heavy and
slow; Riding – light;
Basic – between the
two (the most
popular). Solid
colours, usually
bay or
chestnut.
15-15.2 hh.

Finnish ▶
Works mainly on
farms and in forests
in Finland. Also used
in trotting races and
for riding. Gentle and
alert. Usually
chestnut. Often has
white
markings.
About 15.2 hh.

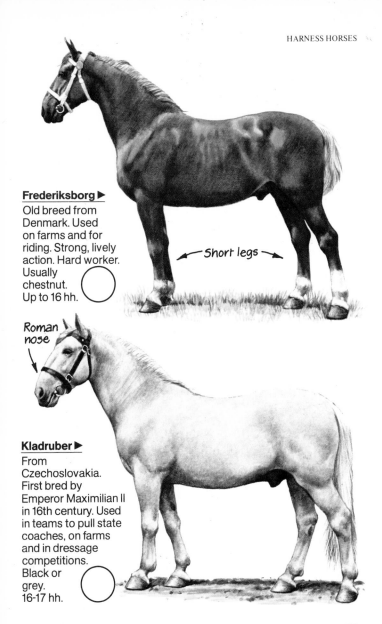

Frederiksborg ▶
Old breed from
Denmark. Used
on farms and for
riding. Strong, lively
action. Hard worker.
Usually
chestnut.
Up to 16 hh.

← Short legs →

Roman
nose

Kladruber ▶
From
Czechoslovakia.
First bred by
Emperor Maximilian II
in 16th century. Used
in teams to pull state
coaches, on farms
and in dressage
competitions.
Black or
grey.
16-17 hh.

Smallish eyes

Nonius ▶
Comes from
Hungary. Named
after Anglo Norman
stallion that founded
the breed. Works on
farms. Black, bay or
brown. Two types:
small – about
15.2 hh;
large –
up to 17 hh.

Light type

◀ Wielkopolski
Popular Polish
breed. Many types:
heavy ones used on
farms; light ones to
drive or ride. Many
bred at state-owned
studs. Usually bay,
brown or
chestnut.
About 16 hh.

40

Draught Horses

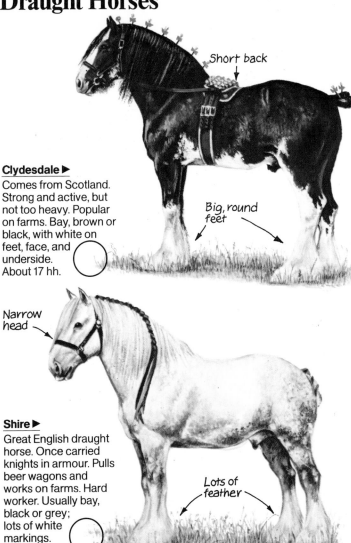

Short back

Clydesdale ▶
Comes from Scotland.
Strong and active, but
not too heavy. Popular
on farms. Bay, brown or
black, with white on
feet, face, and
underside.
About 17 hh.

Big, round
feet

Narrow
head

Shire ▶
Great English draught
horse. Once carried
knights in armour. Pulls
beer wagons and
works on farms. Hard
worker. Usually bay,
black or grey;
lots of white
markings.
Up to 18 hh.

Lots of
feather

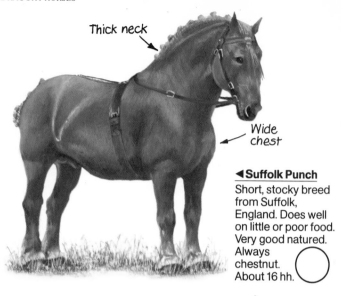

Thick neck

Wide chest

◀ Suffolk Punch

Short, stocky breed from Suffolk, England. Does well on little or poor food. Very good natured. Always chestnut. About 16 hh.

◀ Irish Draught

Good all round farm horse, from Ireland. Makes a top class hunter and jumper if crossed with a Thoroughbred. Often bay; also grey, chestnut or brown. 15.2-16 hh.

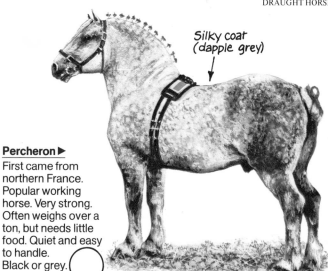

Silky coat
(dapple grey)

Percheron ▶
First came from
northern France.
Popular working
horse. Very strong.
Often weighs over a
ton, but needs little
food. Quiet and easy
to handle.
Black or grey.
15.2-17 hh.

Heavy neck
and shoulders

Ardennes ▶
Ancient breed from
France and Belgium.
Once used by
Napoleon's cavalry.
Powerful and gentle.
Can live out in bad
weather. Usually
roan, bay or
chestnut.
About 15.2 hh.

43

Short head

Dapple grey colour

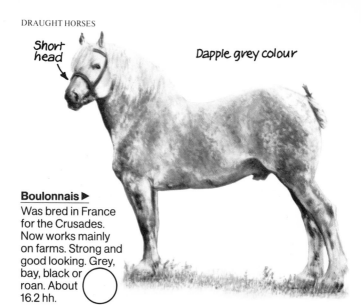

Boulonnais ▶
Was bred in France for the Crusades. Now works mainly on farms. Strong and good looking. Grey, bay, black or roan. About 16.2 hh.

Breton Heavy Draught ▶
Comes from northwest France. Strong, rugged working horse. Related to Postier Breton (carriage horse). Usually strawberry roan, also bay or chestnut. 15-16 hh.

Muscular body

Arched neck

◀ Trait du Nord

Comes from northern France. Breed is being built up; many killed during World War Two. Similar to Ardennes. Quiet and gentle. Usually bay, roan or chestnut. About 16 hh.

◀ Auxois

One of the oldest French breeds. Once used for carriage and farm work. Powerful working horse. Usually bay or strawberry roan. Never black or grey. About 15.2 hh.

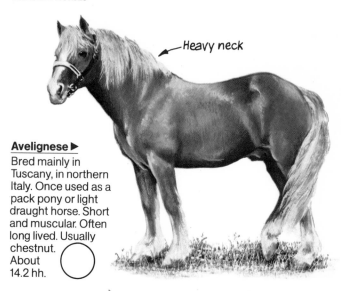

Heavy neck

Avelignese ▶
Bred mainly in
Tuscany, in northern
Italy. Once used as a
pack pony or light
draught horse. Short
and muscular. Often
long lived. Usually
chestnut.
About
14.2 hh.

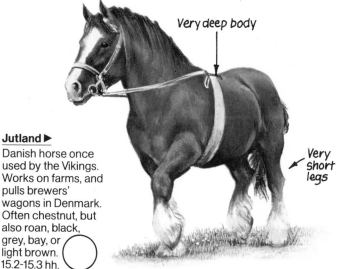

Very deep body

Jutland ▶
Danish horse once
used by the Vikings.
Works on farms, and
pulls brewers'
wagons in Denmark.
Often chestnut, but
also roan, black,
grey, bay, or
light brown.
15.2-15.3 hh.

Very
short
legs

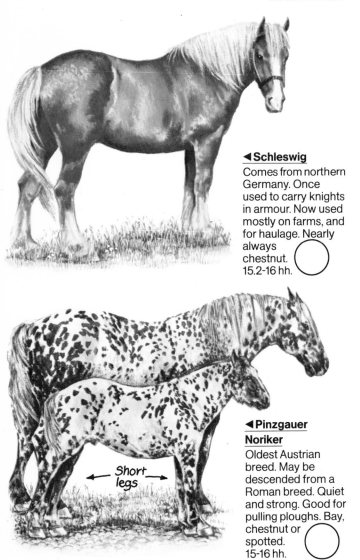

◀ Schleswig

Comes from northern Germany. Once used to carry knights in armour. Now used mostly on farms, and for haulage. Nearly always chestnut. 15.2-16 hh.

Short legs

◀ Pinzgauer Noriker

Oldest Austrian breed. May be descended from a Roman breed. Quiet and strong. Good for pulling ploughs. Bay, chestnut or spotted. 15-16 hh.

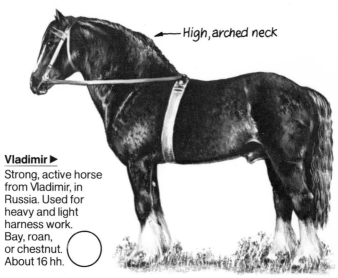

← High, arched neck

Vladimir ▶
Strong, active horse from Vladimir, in Russia. Used for heavy and light harness work. Bay, roan, or chestnut. About 16 hh.

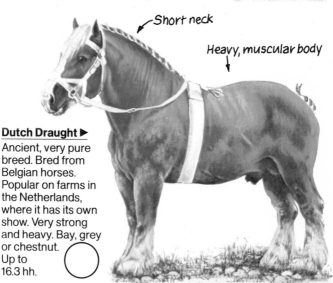

← Short neck

Heavy, muscular body ↓

Dutch Draught ▶
Ancient, very pure breed. Bred from Belgian horses. Popular on farms in the Netherlands, where it has its own show. Very strong and heavy. Bay, grey or chestnut. Up to 16.3 hh.

Points of the horse

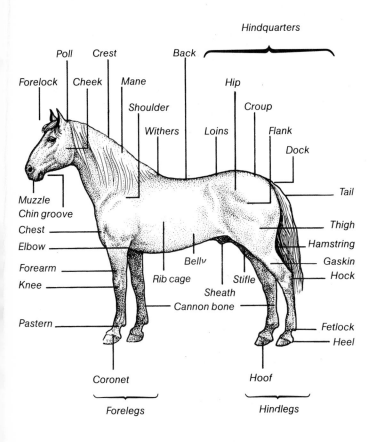

Poll · Crest · Back · Hindquarters
Forelock · Cheek · Mane · Hip
Shoulder · Croup
Withers · Loins · Flank
Dock

Muzzle
Chin groove
Chest
Elbow
Forearm
Knee
Pastern

Rib cage · Belly · Stifle · Sheath · Cannon bone

Coronet

Forelegs

Tail
Thigh
Hamstring
Gaskin
Hock

Fetlock
Heel

Hoof

Hindlegs

Looking after a pony

Keeping a pony in a field

In the wild, ponies live in herds; they move about a great deal, grazing and drinking, and rest for only a few hours at night. There are many things they may miss in captivity. If you keep your pony in a field, try to give it:

- Other horses or ponies to keep it company.
- Good grazing. Each pony needs at least one acre of good grass. You may need to change fields in spring or autumn, to let the grass grow again. Pick up droppings to stop worms from spreading.
- Plenty of fresh water to drink.
- Shelter. Trees, a thick hedge or a shed. Keep a salt or mineral block in the shed.
- Strong fencing. A post and rail wood fence is best. Wire is alright if it is tightly fixed to strong posts with the bottom wire 45 centimetres from the ground.

Thick hedge or shed for shelter

Constant supply of fresh water

Other horses or ponies for company

Strong post and rail fence

Keeping a pony in a stable

It isn't natural for ponies to live indoors. If you keep your pony in a stable, it will need special care. You must do the following things:

● Exercise your pony every day. Ride it for at least one hour, or turn it out in a field for a few hours.

● Give it the right sort of food. A pony needs plenty of bulk food, like hay, to nibble during the day and night. It also needs short food, like corn, in small amounts, in the morning, at night, and perhaps at mid-day.

● Make sure it always has plenty of fresh water.

Stable equipment

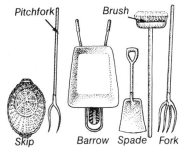

Pitchfork Brush

Skip Barrow Spade Fork

● Muck out the stable every morning. Clear out wet straw and droppings to stop bad smells and thrush (foot disease). Add fresh bedding of straw, wood shavings, peat or sawdust. The bed must be thick enough to keep the pony warm and stop it hurting itself. Pick up droppings at night, too.

● Groom your pony every day. This will keep its coat clean and its skin healthy.

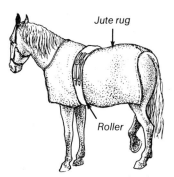

Jute rug

Roller

● Keep your pony warm in winter. If it has a full coat, a jute rug will be enough. If it has been clipped, it will need blankets under the rug as well.

● Let fresh air into the stable to stop your pony getting coughs and colds. Leave the top door open unless it is bitterly cold. To avoid draughts, it is best if the window and door are on the same side of the stable.

If you want to alter your pony's feeding or exercise pattern, do it gradually. Ponies need time to get used to new routines.

Leave top door open

Feeding

What a pony eats

In its natural environment, a pony eats small amounts of bulk food (mostly grass) almost non-stop throughout the day. A pony kept in a stable eats hay instead of grass. The best type of hay to feed your pony is meadow or mixture hay.

If you keep your pony in a field, it may need no extra food during the summer, providing there is plenty of good grass. During the winter, when the grass has stopped growing and is very poor, your pony may need up to six kilograms of hay a day, and even more in frosty or snowy weather.

As well as grass or hay, a pony may need high protein "short" feeds. These are a mixture of corn or cubes and a bulk food like bran or chaff.

You can use these foods to make up a short feed for your pony:

● Corn – Oats or barley. Use crushed or split oats rather than whole oats. Don't give oats to small or excitable ponies. Barley is more fattening but has less food value than oats. Use either crushed barley, or whole barley boiled for two to three hours.

● Cubes – Animal food firms sell different kinds of cubes (also called "nuts"). Read the feeding instructions on the sack carefully.

● Bran – Mix bran into a feed with corn or cubes. It will make your pony eat more slowly and digest its food better.

● Chaff – Chopped hay. Use chaff in the same way as bran.

● Flaked maize – A rich and rather fattening food, unsuitable for small ponies.

● Sugar beet – Good for fattening ponies up. Soak it in water for 24 hours before feeding.

● Linseed – Occasionally give your pony small amounts of boiled linseed; it has good food value and will improve your pony's coat.

● Vegetables – If there is no grass, give your pony fresh root vegetables, or green leaves like sprouts or cabbage leaves. Slice carrots, mangolds, turnips and parsnips lengthwise before adding them to the feed.

Remember to leave a salt or mineral lick (block) in your pony's field or stable.

Haynet

▲ Put hay in a rack or haynet to prevent it being wasted.

Bin

▲ Put short feeds in a manger or galvanized bin.

How to feed a pony

These are the basic rules for feeding a pony:
- Make sure your pony always has enough grass or hay to eat.
- Feed your pony little and often. Ponies have small stomachs, so they can't digest large meals properly.
- Give your pony water to drink before you feed it, not afterwards.
- Never ride your pony straight after a feed; wait about an hour.
- Feed your pony at the same time every day.

Each pony will need different amounts of different kinds of food. What you feed your pony will depend on its temperament, size and health, how much work it has to do, the time of year, where the pony is kept, how much good grass is available, and how much the pony has to eat to keep its weight up.

The table below will give you an idea of what you might feed an average 14 hh pony in one day, at different times of the year.

Table showing approximate daily feeds for an average 14 hh pony				
SEASON	Summer	Summer	Winter	Winter
WHERE KEPT	Field	Field	Stable	Stable
WORK	Light riding	Daily training and shows	Light riding	Daily exercise and hunting
EARLY MORNING		1 kg cubes (if the pony is worked very hard)	3 kg hay	2 kg hay, ½ kg oats, ½ kg cubes, ½-1 kg bran or chaff dampened with water
MID-DAY				2 kg hay, ½ kg oats, ½ kg cubes, ½-1 kg bran or chaff dampened with water
EVENING	½-1 kg cubes (if there is too little good grass)	1-1½ kg oats, ½-1 kg bran or chaff dampened with water	2 kg hay, 1-2 kg oats, ½-1 kg bran or chaff ¼ kg sugar beet (weigh before soaking) ½-1 kg fresh vegetables	2 kg hay, ½-1 kg oats, ¼ kg flaked maize, ¼ kg sugar beet (weigh before soaking), ½-1 kg fresh vegetables

Grooming

You must groom your pony every day if it is kept in a stable.

Pick out its feet with a hoof pick, pulling the pick from heel to toe.

If your pony has a full coat, take off dirt and stains with a dandy brush, working back from the top of its neck. Always brush in the direction the coat lies.

Next, clean its skin and coat with the body brush. This brush has short, soft hairs. Clean the brush by pulling it across a metal or rubber currycomb. Brush the pony's head with the body brush, too, taking care not to knock it. The body brush is also used to brush its mane and tail. If you comb its mane with a mane comb, do it carefully, as it will break the hairs very easily.

Clean its eyes, nostrils and dock with a damp sponge.

Brush round and under its hooves with hoof oil.

Wipe it all over with a clean cloth to make its coat gleam; as a finishing touch, smooth down its mane and tail with a damp brush.

Hoof pick

Dandy brush

Body brush

Metal currycomb

Rubber currycomb

Mane comb

Hoof oil and brush

Sponge and bucket

Cloth

Shoeing

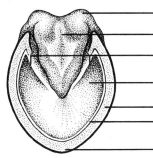

Parts of the hoof

Heel – Back of hoof

Frog – Acts as a cushion

Bars – Where the wall turns in

Sole – Guards the foot, but can become bruised

Wall – Nail-like, no feeling

White line – Between feeling and non-feeling parts of hoof

Toe – Front of hoof

Most working horses and ponies need to wear metal horseshoes, to stop their feet getting worn down. Shoes also stop the hoof becoming cracked, bruised or out of shape.

If your pony works a lot, it will need new shoes every six weeks. In that time, the shoes may wear smooth, and the pony's feet will grow out of them.

Horseshoes must be made to fit properly. The blacksmith or farrier takes the old shoe off first. Then he trims down the wall of the hoof, and fits a new shoe. He can make it fit better if it is hot and pliable. The shoe is nailed to the wall of the hoof where it won't hurt the pony. Finally, the blacksmith files the surface of the shoe smooth.

Riding

A horse has to be carefully prepared before it is ready to be ridden. This is known as "breaking" and "schooling". The horse has to get used to having a rider on its back, and must learn to obey commands. A horse can be broken for riding when it is three years old, and will have an active life until it is 20, if well cared for. (Horses normally live for 25 to 30 years.)

A rider has just as much to learn as a horse does. He must learn to sit so that the horse is well balanced and can move freely. He must also learn to give the horse signals it can understand.

If you want to learn to ride, find a riding school that is approved by horse societies, so you can be sure your teacher is a good one. You should be given a quiet, well schooled horse or pony to begin on.

These are the aids a rider uses to control his horse:

Hands—These hold the reins which control the bit. The bit lies on a sensitive part of the horse's jaw, so you must keep a steady but gentle contact with the bit. Use your hands to slow your horse down, and to turn it to right and left.

Legs – Use your lower leg and heel to make your horse move forward, and turn properly (bending its spine). Your legs should be close to the horse's body. Your heels should be pushed down. If the horse moves suddenly, keep your balance by gripping the saddle with your

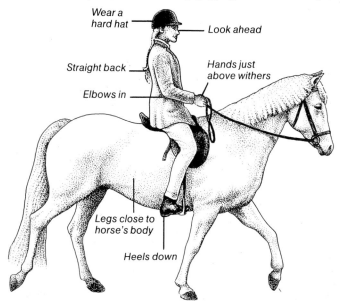

Wear a hard hat

Look ahead

Straight back

Hands just above withers

Elbows in

Legs close to horse's body

Heels down

thighs and knees.

Body – Body weight can be used to drive the horse forward. If you want to slow down, let your weight sink into the saddle. The horse will easily keep its balance if you sit correctly. The legs and reins are all that is needed to change direction.

Voice – Horses have very sharp hearing, and can learn to recognize many sounds. To encourage your horse to move forward, click your tongue. A slow, quiet "Whoa . . ." used with proper seat and rein movements, will steady it down. Never scream or shout near a horse. This will frighten it and it may bolt.

Tack

Good tack (saddles and bridles) is very important. A plain snaffle bridle is best for most ponies. Fit the bridle carefully; ask someone to help you adjust it to fit your pony if you aren't sure how to do it.

For ordinary riding, a general purpose saddle is best. The saddle sits on the pony's back, just behind the withers; it should be well clear of the pony's spine at all times.

Tack is made of leather. You should clean your tack every time you use it, to prevent it becoming hard, and cracking. Clean it with a damp sponge first, then saddle soap it to keep it soft.

General purpose saddle

Snaffle bridle

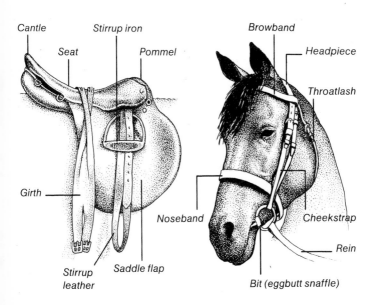

General purpose saddle: Cantle, Stirrup iron, Seat, Pommel, Girth, Stirrup leather, Saddle flap

Snaffle bridle: Browband, Headpiece, Throatlash, Noseband, Cheekstrap, Rein, Bit (eggbutt snaffle)

Glossary

All rounder – horse or pony that is good at different things, like jumping, hunting and gymkhana games.

Cob – short, stocky horse (not more than 15.3 hh). Quiet and well behaved.

Colt – male horse up to three years old.

Dressage – the training of a horse. It includes breaking and basic schooling, as well as the more difficult precision movements that are performed by well-schooled, obedient horses.

Event horse – used in horse trials, which include dressage, show jumping and cross-country riding.

Filly – female horse up to three years old.

Flat racing – racing over short courses without jumps.

Foal – male or female horse up to one year old.

Gelding – male horse that has been de-sexed.

Gymkhana – show where mounted games, like bending and sack races, are held.

Hack – well behaved, well schooled riding horse of light build. Some women ride hacks side-saddle.

Hunter – horse that can gallop cross-country and jump well. It must be strong and very fit.

Hurdler – horse that races and jumps hurdles, usually over courses about four kilometres long.

Mare – female horse more than three years old.

Point-to-point – amateur jumping races. They used to be run from one church steeple (point) to the next.

School master – old, well behaved,

In this gymkhana race, riders lose marks if they spill water

58

well schooled horse or pony. Safe and reliable for people learning to ride.

Show jumping – jumping competitions.

Show horse/pony – competes at shows in various classes, like "Working Hunter" or "Children's Riding Pony". Judged on its appearance, schooling and suitability for the class entered.

Stallion – male horse more than three years old. Usually kept only for breeding.

Steeplechase – race run over fences on courses about eight kilometres long.

Trotter – horse or pony that races in harness; it may either trot or "pace" (move the fore and hind legs on each side together).

Hunter

Mare and foal

Riding holidays

There are various kinds of riding holidays; some teach special skills, like show jumping or dressage, and others cater for people who just want to go pony trekking in the country. Before you go on one, you should have several one-hour riding lessons. You can find out about riding holidays by looking through pony and horse magazines. Try to pick one that is approved by a horse society.

Pony trekking

You don't need a great deal of experience if you want to go on a pony trekking holiday at a trekking centre. You will be given a pony to ride, and you will have to feed and groom it yourself. You will go on a longer ride every day, finishing up with a whole day's ride on the last day of your stay.

Some riding schools run courses lasting anything from a couple of days to a few weeks. The pupils usually stay in lodgings near the school. If you go on one of these courses, you may have lessons in the morning, and relax in the afternoon, often with gymkhana games. Branches of the Pony Club run summer camps lasting about a week. At camp, you will learn more about riding, jumping and pony care. The camp may finish off with a small show or gymkhana. If you don't own a pony, you may be able to hire one from a riding stable for a week.

Pony Club camp

Clubs to join

The best club to join is the *Pony Club*, which is part of the *British Horse Society*; both are based at the National Equestrian Centre, Stoneleigh, Kenilworth, Warwickshire. Anyone under 20 years of age can join this club. It has branches all over Britain, and organizes many activities, including summer camps, inter-branch competitions, visits to kennels and stud farms, and horse shows. It also provides instruction on riding, pony care and saddlery. Write to the headquarters (Stoneleigh) to find out where your nearest branch is.

There are various other clubs you can join, including the *Horse Rangers*, Royal Mews, Hampton Court, Middlesex; this is a club for children who don't have their own ponies. It has stables in and around London. Riding schools sometimes run clubs for children learning to ride. Ask at your local riding school for information.

Useful addresses

Association of British Riding Schools, Chesham House, 56 Green End Road, Sawtry, Huntingdon.
British Driving Society, 10 Marley Avenue, New Milton, Hampshire.
British Show Pony Society, Smale Farm, Wisborough Green, Billingshurst, Sussex.

British Veterinary Society, 7 Mansfield Street, Portland Place, London W1.
National Pony Society, Stoke Lodge, 85 Cliddesden Road, Basingstoke, Hampshire.
Ponies of Britain, Brookside Farm, Ascot, Berkshire.

Books to read

The Manual of Horsemanship. (British Horse Society). A must. No-nonsense textbook.
Keeping a Pony at Grass. (Pony Club). Lots of practical advice.
Children's Encyclopaedia of Horses & Ponies. C. Rawson, J. Spector, E. Polling (Usborne). Illustrated international guide.
Summerhays' Encyclopaedia for Horsemen. (Frederick Warne). Old and respected reference book; has been updated.
The Encyclopedia of the Horse. (Ebury Press/Pelham). Large, detailed and fairly expensive.
Caring for your Pony. N. Fenner (W. & G. Foyle Ltd). Lots of common sense.
Feeding Ponies. W. Miller (J. A. Allen & Co.) How, why and what to feed.
Horses and Riding. B. Skelton (Stanley Paul). Packed with first-class advice and ideas.
The Young Rider's Companion. G. Wheatley (William Luscombe). Good all round handbook.

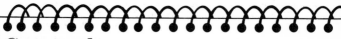

Scorecard

The horses and ponies on this scorecard are arranged in alphabetical order. When you see one, write down the date in the blank space next to each name and circle your score. You can add up your score after a day at a horse show, for instance.

	Score	Date seen		Score	Date seen
Akhal-Teke	25		Dartmoor	5	
American Saddlebred	20		Døle	25	
Andalusian	15		Don	25	
Anglo-Arab	10		Dutch Draught	15	
Anglo Norman	20		Exmoor	5	
Appaloosa	15	✓	Falabella	20	
Arab (any type)	10		Fell	10	
Ardennes	15		Finnish	20	
Auxois	20		Fjord	15	
Avelignese	20		Fredericksborg	20	
Barb	20		Friesian	20	
Boulonnais	20		Gelderlander	15	
Breton	15		Gotland	20	
Budyonny	25		Groningen	20	
Camargue	15		Hackney	5	
Caspian	25		Haflinger	15	
Cleveland Bay	10		Hanoverian	15	
Clydesdale	10	✓	Highland	5	✓
Connemara	5		Holstein	15	
Criollo	25		Huçul	25	
Dale	10		Icelandic	20	

	Score	Date seen		Score	Date seen
Irish Draught	10		Shire	5	
Jutland	20		Standardbred	15	
Karabair	25		Suffolk Punch	10	
Kazakh	25		Tarpan	25	
Kladruber	25		Tennesee Walking Horse	20	
Knabstrup	20		Thoroughbred	5	✓
Kustanair	25		Trait du Nord	20	
Lipizzaner	15		Trakehner	15	
Lusitano	20		Turkoman	25	
Morgan	20		Vladimir	20	
New Forest	5		Waler	20	
Nonius	25		Welsh Cob	10	
Oldenburger	15		Welsh Mountain	5	✓
Orlov Trotter	25		Wielkopolski	20	
Palomino	10	✓			
Paso Fino	20				
Percheron	15				
Pinto	10				
Pinzgauer Noriker	25				
Pony of the Americas	20				
Przewalski	20				
Quarter Horse	15				
Sable Island	25				
Schleswig	15				
Shetland	5	✓			

Index